Swimming with Dolphins

GREAT STORY & COOL FACTS

Introduction

Welcome to Half and Half books, a great combination of story and facts! You might want to read this book on your own. However, the section with real facts is a little more difficult to read than the story. You might find it helpful to read the facts section with your parent, or someone else, who can help you with the more difficult words. Your parent may also be able to answer any questions you have about the facts—or at least help you find more information!

Swimming with Dolphins

English Edition Copyright © 2010 by Treasure Bay, Inc.
English Edition translated by Elizabeth Bell
and edited by Editorial Services of Los Angeles

Original Edition: S.O.S. Dauphin
Copyright © 2001 by Nathan VUEF, Paris—France

S.O.S. Dolphin by Laurence Gillot
Illustrated by Rocco

Nonfiction text by Elisabeth Sébaoun
Nonfiction Illustrations by Gaëtan Dorémus

Photography Credits: F. Stuart Westmorland/La Photothèque SDP,
Gérard Soury/Jacana, Varin Visage/Jacana, Norbert Wu/Jacana, Grinberg/Jacana

Special thanks to Doreen Moser Gurrola, Marine Science Instructor
at The Marine Mammal Center in Sausalito, California,
for her suggestions and review of the information in this book.

Published by
Treasure Bay, Inc.
P.O. Box 119
Novato, CA 94948

Printed in Singapore

Library of Congress Catalog Card Number: 2009932094

Hardcover ISBN-13: 978-1-60115-215-2
Paperback ISBN-13: 978-1-60115-216-9

Visit us online at:
www.HalfAndHalfBooks.com

Swimming with Dolphins

CONTENTS

Story: S.O.S. Dolphin   2

What's the Order?   17

Facts: About Dolphins

Tell Me about Yourself   18

What Do You Do All Day?   20

Are There Any Dangers?   22

What about Baby Dolphins?   24

How Do Dolphins Communicate?   26

Making Waves   28

Dolphin Tales   29

S.O.S. Dolphin

by **Laurence Gillot**
Illustrated by **Rocco**

"Swim close to me," said Pablo's dad,
putting on his snorkel mask. "And when
I give the signal, we dive. Got it?"

"Okaaaaaaay!" Pablo replied, his voice muffled in his snorkel mask.

Pablo and his dad dove into the warm ocean water. It was clear and blue, with bright, colorful fish swimming in schools below them. The view was incredible!

Pablo loved going on underwater adventures with his dad. He always showed Pablo lots of cool things, like odd-looking shells and fish that were hiding.

While they were exploring, Pablo suddenly felt a tap on his leg. It was the signal! Pablo took a deep breath and dipped his head under the water like a duck.

His dad pointed to a starfish in the sand. He picked it up and put it in Pablo's hand. Suddenly, he grabbed Pablo's arm and pointed his finger toward . . .

"A dolphin!" thought Pablo.

The dolphin was coming toward them. It was gigantic compared to Pablo! His dad quickly pulled up Pablo toward the surface of the water.

As their heads popped up out of the water, they heard short, piercing cries: "EEEE! EEEE! EEEE!"

It was the dolphin talking! It was so close that Pablo could see its huge head. Its teeth looked sharp. Pablo felt scared.

His dad seemed a bit worried, too. Pulling up his snorkel, he said, "Normally, a dolphin will not attack humans, but safety comes first! Let's go back toward the beach!"

As they swam, Pablo looked back. The dolphin was following them!

"What if it takes a bite out of my leg?" Pablo wondered. The thought made him panic, and he kicked his flippers faster and faster.

"I can touch bottom!" called out his dad.

Feeling like he could barely breathe, Pablo kicked the last few feet to his dad.

The dolphin jumped up out of the water. "EEEE! EEEE! EEEE!" it said, wagging its head back and forth.

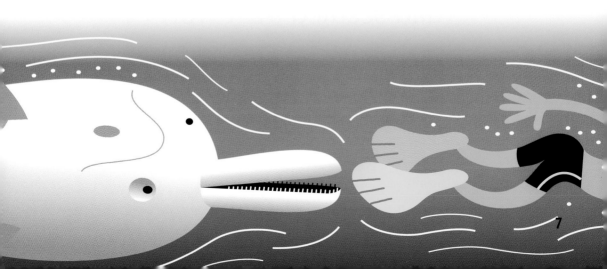

"It looks like it wants to tell us something," Pablo's dad whispered.

"It's diving! It's coming right at us!" Pablo yelled.

Pablo and his dad stood there, frozen, as the dolphin got closer and closer and . . . then was at their feet, pushing at his dad's legs with its snout.

Pablo suddenly understood what the dolphin wanted. "It wants us to follow it!" Pablo cried. Then, without thinking, he grabbed onto its top fin and away they went!

"Pablo!" his dad cried. "Let go!"

It was too late! The dolphin swam away—with Pablo on it! It seemed to know exactly where it was going.

The dolphin zoomed through the waves. Pablo was panting hard. He did not know whether to panic or laugh! He could feel the dolphin's smooth skin under his hands. Pablo's heart beat like a drum.

Pablo's dad was on the shore. He was running like a crazy person, waving his arms in the air, trying to follow them.

The dolphin turned and swam onto the beach. There, on the sand, was a small dolphin!

Pablo got off the dolphin and moved closer. The little dolphin was stranded between two rocks!

Pablo realized it must be her baby! Peering closer, he noticed that the baby had something in its mouth.

Pablo ripped off his diving mask and bent down close to the little animal. A piece of rusty metal was stuck in its jaws.

"Ouch!" Pablo whispered to the baby. "That must hurt, poor fella."

Just then Pablo's dad caught up. He looked very upset. "Pablo! Are you all right?" he said.

"Yes, I'm OK. But this baby dolphin is not!" he replied.

His dad bent down to look. "With that piece of junk stuck in its mouth, it can't eat," he said. "The poor little thing is weak. Maybe that's why it got stuck here."

Very carefully and gently, his dad got the metal out of the baby dolphin's mouth.

"Come on!" he said to Pablo. "Let's get it out of here! You take the head, and I'll take the tail."

Pablo put his arms around the baby dolphin's neck. He whispered softly to it, "Don't worry, little fella! You're going to be okay."

The baby dolphin opened its eyes!

Pablo smiled and kept talking gently, "You can do this!"

His dad said, "Ready? On the count of three, we lift! One, two, three!"

The baby dolphin was heavy, but they lugged it into the water.

Mama dolphin came right up and nuzzled her head against her baby's. But the young dolphin still did not move. She rubbed and rubbed. The baby finally began to stir. Pablo knew at that moment that it would be OK!

He was so happy and proud. Pablo hugged his dad.

"You did great, son!" said Pablo's dad. "Now it's time to go back. They don't need us anymore."

Pablo and his dad jumped back in the ocean. They swam and swam. A loud splash behind them made them look back.

Their two new friends burst through the waves! They were both swimming! They jumped. They splashed!

"EEEE! EEEE!" They were saying goodbye to Pablo and his dad.

Then the two dolphins headed out to the wide, open sea.

The End

What's the Order?

In which order do these events happen in the story?

I'm a dolphin!
I have lungs and a spine
like cats, dogs, and humans.

I can stay underwater for 10 to
15 minutes without breathing.
Then I go back up to the surface
to take a big gulp of air.

There is a little opening at the top
of my head. It is called a *blowhole*.
It allows me to breathe when I
come up out of the water. When I
dive, the blowhole closes.

I live in the sea, just like fish do. But I am not a fish. I am a mammal!

I am a sea mammal.

My skin is very soft, I love to be stroked, and I can hear very well.

Under my skin, I have a layer of fat to keep my blood warm.

Oh, I'm very busy! First of all, I'm never alone. I always swim with my friends in a group called a pod. Together we frolic and play. We love to have fun.

When we're hungry, we hunt. Watch out, we swim very fast! It comes in handy when we're chasing schools of fish.

If one of us gets hurt, a friend helps the wounded one stay on the surface. Otherwise we could sink and drown!

Do All Day?

There are many different kinds of dolphins, including:

Risso's dolphin

bottlenose dolphin

pilot whale

Yes, it's really a type of dolphin, even though it's called a pilot whale!

Dolphins belong to the animal family called **Delphinidae** [del-FIN-uh-day].

Dolphins also belong in the animal order of **cetaceans** [suh-TAY-shins], which includes whales such as:

sperm whale
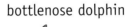

gray whale

beluga whale

Other mammals that live in the sea include:

seal

walrus

Before it is born, a baby dolphin grows in its mother's belly. Dolphin babies are born in the water, of course!

When she is ready to give birth, the mother dolphin leaves the pod with another female dolphin known as the auntie.

What about Baby

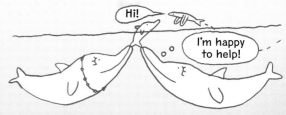

When the baby is born, the tail comes out first, the head last. And as soon as it is completely out . . .

. . . the auntie and the mother quickly help the baby up to the surface so it can breathe. They have to hurry so it does not drown!

How do they survive?

A mother dolphin keeps a close eye on her baby. She never leaves it alone. Her little one always swims by her side.

And if she has to go off to find food, she leaves the baby in the auntie's care.

The little dolphin needs its mother. It nurses on her milk for one or two years. It will not eat fish until it is six months old.

Dolphins?

How Do Dolphins

Did you know that dolphins are very intelligent? They can even communicate with one another.

Dolphins do not have lips and voice boxes to make words like we do. But they can make whistles that sound like clicks, moans, trills, grunts, and creaks.

Echolocation

Dolphins also have a cool skill, similar to sonar, called **echolocation** [eh-koe-low-KAY-shin].

Dolphins make clicking noises. These clicks create underwater sound waves. The waves bounce off objects, like animals swimming in the ocean, and bounce back to the dolphin. Listening to these bouncing sound waves helps the dolphin figure out what and where the object is.

Echolocation also helps dolphins find food or know when enemies are near.

Communicate?

Signature whistles

A dolphin's whistle is like a fingerprint; each dolphin has one of its very own, called a **signature whistle**.

When a baby dolphin is born, its mother whistles a lot to the baby so that it will learn the mother's special whistle.

Sometime between one and six months of age, a dolphin starts making its own signature whistle.

Dolphins listen to one another's signature whistles, and then they whistle back, or go find out what the whistling dolphin wants.

Dolphins in trouble make their signature whistles very loudly.

Making Waves

Sonar stands for **So**und **n**avigation **a**nd **r**anging. Like echolocation, sonar uses sound and echoes to find things underwater. Submarines use sonar just like dolphins use echolocation.

Sound waves bounce off objects. When sound waves are underwater, sometimes you can actually feel the waves.

Want to see how this works?

Needed: A parent   Bathtub or kitchen sink
          Cookie sheet   with about 10 to 12
          Hammer   inches of water

1. At one end of the bathtub or sink, have your parent hold the cookie sheet and the hammer under water. (Both must be under water.) Put your hand in the water at the other end.

2. Have your parent tap the hammer gently against the cookie sheet. Try to feel the underwater sound wave with your hand.

3. You can also use two cookie sheets, one on each side. Experiment with the wave strength while holding the sheets at different levels in the water. Each time the waves might feel different.

Dolphin Tales

There are many stories about dolphins rescuing humans at sea.

It has been said that a pod of dolphins saved two fishermen by pushing their broken boat all the way to shore—with them in it! Dolphins have even led people lost at sea to safety.

Dolphins have a special place in our histories and our hearts, not only for their intelligence, but also for their apparent kindness.

Perhaps someday, scientists and dolphins will be able to communicate better with each other. If that happens, we may be able to learn a lot more about dolphins—and maybe they can learn more about us!

If you liked *Swimming with Dolphins,* here is another Half and Half™ book you are sure to enjoy!

A Doctor for the Animals

STORY: Julie loves all kinds of animals. She loves dogs and cats and horses and fish. One day, she finds a bird that has been hurt. Maybe she can help the bird by taking it to the veterinarian. And maybe, someday, Julie will be a vet herself and help lots of animals.

FACTS: If you like animals, maybe someday you could be a veterinarian! Vets help animals that are sick or hurt. Learn about the different kinds of vets, including city vets, country vets and vets for wild animals! It's all inside and ready for you to explore in this fun-packed book.

To see all the Half and Half books that are available, just go online to **www.HalfandHalfBooks.com**